Whispers of the Soul

MAHITHA ATTILI

ISBN 979-8-89277-622-6

Dedicated to you,
who is broken yet smiles back

CONTENTS

AUTHOR BIO

Through the art of poetry, Mahitha paints images with language, weaving together emotions and imagery in beautifully crafted verses. Whether it's the gentle cadence of nature-inspired poems or the raw intensity of personal reflections, Mahitha's poetry and short stories and thought work evokes a range of feelings, inviting readers to pause, reflect, and connect with the power of language and human touch.

FOREWORD

Whispers of the Soul" is a captivating collection that weaves together the beauty of poetry, the power of short stories, and the inspiring wisdom of motivational thoughts. Within these pages, readers will embark on a transformative journey that touches the depths of their hearts and stirs their souls.

In the realm of poetry, the author explores the myriad emotions and experiences that shape our lives. Through evocative verses

and poignant imagery, they delve into themes of love, loss, hope, and resilience.

Each poem becomes a window into the human spirit, offering solace, reflection, and moments of profound connection.

Interspersed throughout the collection are captivating short stories, each one a gem that transports readers to diverse worlds and compelling narratives. From tales of redemption and self-discovery to intriguing mysteries and heartfelt relationships, these stories invite readers to contemplate the complexities of the human condition and the infinite possibilities that exist within us all.

Complementing the poetry and short stories are motivational thoughts that serve as beacons of inspiration. Drawing from personal experiences, the author shares insightful reflections on overcoming challenges, embracing self-belief, and finding the strength to pursue dreams. These empowering thoughts ignite the reader's inner fire and encourage them to embrace their own potential.

As readers immerse themselves in the pages of "Whispers of the Soul," they will find themselves transported to a realm where words paint vivid pictures, emotions dance across the page, and inspiration ignites the spirit. This collection serves as a reminder that within every soul lies a tapestry of stories, poetry, and thoughts waiting to be shared and cherished.

With its blend of lyrical poetry, captivating short stories, and uplifting motivational thoughts, "Whispers of the Soul" is a literary treasure that invites readers to explore the depths of their own hearts, find solace in shared experiences, and embark on a transformative journey of self-discover.

FAILED LOVE

Nestled among rolling hills, there existed a love story that was destined for greatness. It was a tale of two souls intertwined in a bond so strong, it could withstand any storm. But little did they know that their love would be tested by the very people who were supposed to protect and nurture it.

Meet Emily, a vibrant and free-spirited young woman with an infectious laughter that could light up even the darkest room. And then there was Ethan, a kind-hearted and ambitious young man with dreams as vast as the sky. Their paths crossed one sunny afternoon, and from that moment on, they became inseparable.

Their love blossomed like a beautiful garden, filling their hearts with joy and hope. However, fate had other plans. The news of their relationship reached the ears of their parents, and they were less than thrilled. Unbeknownst to Emily and Ethan, their parents held a deep-seated rivalry that spanned generations. They were determined to separate the two lovers, and they would stop at nothing to achieve their goal.

With every passing day, their parents began to manipulate their lives, planting seeds of doubt and mistrust in their hearts. They poisoned their minds with false stories and exaggerated truths, painting a picture that showcased their partner in a negative light. Slowly, the walls that once protected their love began to crumble.Emily, tormented by thoughts of betrayal, decided to confront Ethan one fateful evening. Tears streaming down her face, she poured out her heart and accused him of being disloyal. Ethan, equally devastated, denied the accusations vehemently.

In their pain and confusion, both chose to believe what they were told about each other, fueling the growing distance between them.Years passed, and their love story became a distant memory. Emily and Ethan, once inseparable lovers, had become bitter enemies. They resented one another, their hearts filled with regret and anger. But deep down, a flicker of curiosity remained, a longing to know the truth that had been buried under layers of deceit.And so, fate intervened once more. Emily, now a successful writer, stumbled upon a box filled with old letters and photographs. As she sifted through the remnants of their shattered love, the truth began to emerge.

The letters told a different story, one that shattered the illusions created by their parents. It was a story of undying love, of sacrifices made in the name of their forbidden union.Emily's heart ached with the weight of realisation. She knew that she had to find Ethan and set things right. With determination burning in her eyes, she tracked him down to a small café on the outskirts of town. And there he was, sitting alone, sipping his coffee with a melancholic gaze.Their eyes met, and in that moment, time stood still. Words were unnecessary as their hearts spoke a language only they could understand. The pain and regret melted away, leaving only love and forgiveness in its wake.But just as they were about to embrace, the story took an unexpected turn. The café door swung open, and there stood their parents, the architects of their heartbreak. Their faces etched with sorrow, they confessed to their vile actions, revealing the truth that had been hidden for so long.

The lovers were left standing there, caught between the past and the present, with a future uncertain yet filled with hope. The questions that had haunted them for years were finally answered, but the scars remained, a constant reminder of the love they had lost.And so, dear reader, the story of Emily and Ethan comes to an end, or does it? For in their hearts, a glimmer of possibility still exists. Will they find the strength to rebuild what was lost? Only time will tell, and perhaps, in the end, they will discover that true love can withstand even the harshest of trials.

DARK CLOUDS

The dark clouds with a chilly wind make the trees dance and sing. Welcoming the downpour from the sky when we step out and having a moment with the earth gives us a refreshing and new feel. But the dark clouds I'm talking about are different; they terrify, bother, and never leave you that easily. Have you ever felt dark clouds filling everywhere, along with the hot breeze chilling your spine? Sometimes it feels nothing like you will get numb with the constant pain and struggle. It is not just one feeling that can carry; there may be a million or more.

Getting over it in one day or overnight would be the best dream come true to feel. But I say it never happens unless one masters their mind.

Hearing the words from people that

"We face a lot more than you, look at us, we are all fine",

"it's all in your mind and imagination",

"Don't get controlled by the mind, you should control it",

"it won't get better unless you work to make it better" and many more.

These are not just words that come out of someone's mouth; rather they tend to hurt more. I sometimes felt like saying,

"If you don't know how it feels, prefer not to say anything".

Feeling numb is how it will be. At times, after being in lots of trauma and turmoil on endless floors, 'NUMBness' fills the body and mind. The pain and suffering will be there, an impalpable cloud.

I, feeling not like sharing anything with anyone. Not even good, bad or even worse. Trust goes under the wrap, and bringing it back to life will never be easy. There sends a ray of hope even when you are in the pitch dark. But again, life takes it back and throws you into the dark world and says to find a way out all by yourself again. It fills you, the darkness, sadness or what-so-ever it's named. You can feel it in all your body, mind and soul. It might also be a delusion in terms of great people and scientists. Only the people who go through this can relate to the feeling. The harder you try to get better, the more it goes away. Some say - to be grateful for what you have. At that time, all you can see is the scrambling of the worst things. Even the searching will get back to the worst flashbacks.

All that is visible is the pit holes that life throws you into. Rage anger fills the nerves sometimes. Irritating for unwanted things, feeling impulsive for everything. Unable to tell how the feelings are and why they are coming? It's hard to understand at times. Finding the back reasons and giving alternative thoughts feels impossible at the same time. Controlling and pressing back the anger inside, trying to push them into a dark corner, is the only thing I can do rather than busting out to people how I'm hiding a volcanic rage inside, but inwardly feeling the self-shattering. There was hope for every step I used to take. But later, I watch it falling apart. With all these unsolved puzzles in my life I started seeing life as a knotted rope which started hanging from the ceiling fan, I felt taking a swing by it. But something stopped. I couldn't see as my eyes were shutted tight. It is him.....

PEACH TO RED

It is this beautiful peach rose plant that bags a part of my love everyday; plugged it's thorn and tore my skin two.

The drips of blood from the thorn flowing as the blood in my veins pump...... It seemed like the plant weeps blood and shedded as it need water no more. Making the peach rose to red remind the shatters of pain to hold

Is it the love that made to shed tears of blood

Or

Is it the trust that made blind to thorns?

THE WIND FLIT

The heavy wind lifting up the dead leaves turning and tossing them like a magic adding the dust

I can't see you but feel you and when…

The heavy wind blew the dust on my face like cleansing me with the filth..

HOURGLASS DREAM?

Tapping down The hourglass

when the last sand speckles are dying to come down...

When the rest was leaked down smooth and relish

Turning up to down its filling back inside in another way..... The finger of one is running on the hourglass

It ended as I woke up.

FOR YOU!

Counting days and weeks to see you right next to me...

Feeding the butterflies inside to fly and tingle me to let me know you are the GUY.

Asking my eyes to work some more better to fill him inside so I don't miss carrying him around.

Sweeping the dust of my heart, filling the holes to make it look new and sweet.

Does he feel the same thing I'm storing and feeling...

What if he makes another ditch in my heart.. open my tears and let them flow... Kill the butterflies and never let them be reborn... Million questions arise...

Thanks to my past for not letting me live in magic.

LOVE IN THE AIR

They say love is in the air....

A metaphoric way of love....

But all I know is filling my lungs with the air and releasing some rest... If I can breathe love why couldn't it fill me or is it too big to fit in my nasal XD

THE ACTUAL STROKE

25

You can feel it when the heart crumbles down for things that didn't fit in your small heart rather break through....

The pain is real...

You can feel it....

It feels like something is pulling inside you and making it shatter.... You can feel the heart with high beats wanting to come out into your bare hands to smash it down with, rather being in a cage and taking the slow pills of pain again and again....

Is it really worth it? It has one duty; to pump blood. But why does it even care about it? Why does that get hurt, break down, give an immense pain!

Should I caress it for baring enough... Should I caress it to get better by self....Should I caress it to become a stone....

YOU TO YOU

It's okay to hate.

It's okay to feel bad.

It's okay to have guilt trips again and again.

All that matters to you is you.

ALONE? THEN REMEMBER

It's remembering memories of all the people who left me by what-so-ever reason and made me alone. They're happy and everything with the people who they think they love are too. You did nothing but good to everyone, and it turns out as a lit in your heart. You feel alone while you are running through their status and stuff.

But on a position note - You are enough for you, and you don't have to deal with their toxic nature and unpleasant gossip anymore. You have everything that makes you feel better and engaged. What is the purpose of them being in your life? Were you happy with the way they treated you? Do you even like their attitude? Do you feel comfortable with their criticising jokes and selfish behaviour?

A BIG NO, right? So, it is OK to feel what you are feeling because it's you; who cares all along. It doesn't matter who is with you and who leaves. It's you being happy no matter what, is the only thing that matters. Chill! Girl. You are always loved

by yourself,

remember.

PEACOCK FEATHERS

Does a peacock feel so heavy to drag itself from place to place because of its feathers growing jungle? Do ants ever get tired of searching for food all day and night? And when do these humans stop pretending to be good in every eye and give so much toxicity to everyone? Feeling bad about the way people portrayed someone to others just for whatever shit they wanted to get.

Realising the true colours of people is somewhat of a painful journey. Sometimes it feels like why do I even know them, and for what. Why do I trust people so easily and get hurt later though I know their true colours? I build love in a snap of a moment, and later the heartache gets so real; it actually feels like a real heart stroke. Whether or not I show it out but it takes time to mend it together and get it band-aided. A little change will always impact the whole life, mind and body. The overstressing of things is giving me severe body aches. I told you mental health things impact physical health like anything.

And that is how one can master the term LONELINESS by getting nothing but back stabs and painful paths.

All I did; patting my back and said, "It's ok, dear. It's for good".

That's all even you have to do.

SCARS OF LOVE

I jumped in happiness when he watched me while I walked from afar. I blushed like a rabbit when he hugged me in public. My heart pounded hard when he would speak to me for hours after work. I relished when he filled my wardrobe.

It took a while for my eyes to learn that It was all driven by the shadows of his doubts he was carrying around me.

Oh! stupid me, that is how he made sure that you see no other guy, that is how he made sure that every handsome hunk on the road realises you're his. That is how he made sure that you speak with no other guy than him. That is how he leaves your whole body covered in band-aids and scars. It's not love.

Oh! boy, tell her the truth.

FAREWELL GIRLFRIEND

It was the summer of the 2000s when I bid farewell to my girlfriend, seeking the allure of something new. In turn, she departed from her own partner, finding solace in my embrace. It was all the fresh butterflies fluttering within us filling our bodies.

She was a new magic addition to my life, and I wanted to carry it for the rest of my life. Knotting her with me, we became a brand new married couple among the friends of both with our hearts intertwined.

Yet, in retrospect, all that transpired felt like a grand illusion. The vibrant colours of our romance, the promises and dreams that seemed so tangible. Now appear distant and intangible. It took several months for the truth to unravel, revealing that my girl had not truly moved on from her ex, despite the fact that we had entered into separate relationships.

No matter the chance she took to move on from him, despite the enchantment I tried to create with the magic spells of my love, she chose him.

She chooses him!

She ran away, distancing herself from my heart but remaining close to my surroundings. Taking not just my broken soul but all the earnest things I ever saved.

Every moment she had once spent by my side now felt like a haunting nightmare, and even her shadow, once comforting, now seemed tainted with darkness and deceit.

The memories we had created together, once cherished and cherished, now carried a sinister undertone. Her presence, once a source of comfort and solace, now filled me with a sense of unease and foreboding.

NTH TIME

As the cold breeze hit my skin I got chills on my spine. These chills are never new but not for the breeze.

All a sudden I saw him jumping and dancing like a fool just as in the past. But with another girl.

I saw her.

When he stopped being excited for no reason and held her hand. I saw her.

Her hair is flowing like a slow stream. Pushing back her hair she smiled at him. Her eyes were twinkling as she fell in love for the first time. Her lips are going wide everytime he speaks.

Is he that funny?

She held his hand round her body and he came to her.... They exchanged a peck. And that is where my heart actually broke for the 'n'th time.

IT'S OK

Is it ok to breathe

When everything around you is vaporising up

Is it ok to take a break

When you're exhausted with the crunch of life

Is it ok to not care

When anything and everything can point at you.

OH MY SINGLE ROOM

You live alone with a single cot

And that cuddles with single blanket

The things in it are yours…. So is the pain

Stories are alone…. So are the tears

You hide me between the walls… so do my secrets

You cover me with a shade…. So do my loneliness

Oh my single room… Will you be my valentine

IT IS

It's heavy.... There is nothing to weigh its weight

It's hard.... There is probably nothing that melts it down

It's painful... There is nothing that can kills it

It's hurtful.... There is probably nothing that could band-it out.

CAN I

Can I just flood out in the water

Soaring freely in the air

Delve deep into the earth

and become phoenix from the fire

ROSES

43

We're like roses

We're beautiful

And we've thorns.

SWEET LITTLE SMILE

When my sweet little smile is showing up

Deep inside the dark is unfurling every inch.

When eyes and waving out happiness

Deep inside pumps of tears are piling up

What's wrong?

may be nothing Or May be everything

HATE TO LOVE

There are two words which have a great influence on our life. It shapes the world, it shapes our feelings. We meet hundreds of people in our lives, and we categorise everyone into two 'hate-able' and 'lovable', and for some, no feelings or connections are perceivable; we meet, talk and perish. But, both love and hateable people are special to us.

There are times when we change their category in our lives; love to hate and hate to love. Because feelings are always unstable; we humans are always unbalanced. Unknowingly, we obey some unworthy theories that never serve us a penny but make us weak. Theories like, if someone hates us we hate them if someone cheats, fakes, misguides, tortures, blames or whatever that hurts us can be hated too. And there are many more theories which are beyond a positive thought.

I appreciate the people who love to follow these theories by feeding all the negativity into their brain no matter how good we treat them. They always skim people for mistakes; did anything- hate them, didn't do anything- hate them, love us- still hate them.

They're the real treasure of haterade. I wish they get a proper pamper and love or maybe an awareness on what life is. Of course, I'm too young to talk about such things but yes! I'm sound and young enough to learn to get much awareness of such things. This 'HATE' word is simple enough to ruin our peace and smile. The only medicine for this word is 'LOVE', it's not a curse but a mantra to change our being. It's a positive shift that we give to our haters. Replace the hate with love, then that will be the only thing that girdles you.

Whatever consequences take place in our lives like mentioned before which ends up with hate will happen to change us, to strengthen us, to enlighten us, of how far we can make ourselves a better one. Those consequences are quite common for everyone but differently, cause you're not higher for god or I'm not lesser.

I do have people who I hate. They're the people who ripped me, who made me mentally weak. I never replaced the hate into love for them because the damage is huge. Rather I misplaced them from my life, I killed them in my memories, and I erased their presence in my world. And the rest of whom I have to meet some (or) the other time are being a little complicated yet lovable. Pretending is never my word towards them rather having a snip of positivity when

I face them. And for my private time, I tease them on my way with close pals for my mental happiness ☒.

Might or might not be easy but it changed my perspective.

BEING A WEAK TO BECOME STRONG

In the realm of success, a word renowned,

Yet, its taste is shifty, a rare gem to be found.

With youthful passion, she embarked on her quest,

Unsure if destiny would deem her blessed.

A childhood by illness and woe,

Denied the joys that others came to know.

Recognizing her worth, her strength untold,

Seizing opportunities, a challenge to behold.

Sickness tethered her, fear of failure entwined,

Limiting her chances to prove her own mind.

Oxygen masks and monitors, constant companions,

IV cannulas became part of her and saline, her food.

Sympathy, the emotion she often received,

Injecting self-pity, making her feel deceived.

But overcoming these trials became her aim,

Medicines and care, healing her body's flame.

Self-pity, a burden she gradually shed,

Replacing it with resilience, strength instead.

In the realm of studies, an unsettling test,

A devilish challenge that left her unrested.

But every setback, a lesson in disguise,

Training her to rise, reaching for the skies.

For everything happens with purpose in sight,

To mould, empower us, to change our plight

She embraced the journey of learning and growth,

Conquering weaknesses, unveiling her faith.

Transformed by the lessons of her past,

Self-acceptance kindling a love unsurpassed within.

No longer trapped in self-blame's cruel game,

Acceptance granted her freedom, a life untamed.

And thus, the game of life began to unfold,

A testament to resilience, a story yet untold

STONE SOUL

The hands held me tight when I was walking away

The smooth touch said it all, while the love in those eyes carry

But I took the heart out and broke it into million pieces

And watched the eyes soak in wet

Remembering that only love is not enough

I place a stone inside my soul.

ANXIETY

Sometimes unknowing, u pick your skin

You bite your nails without a habit

Pull your fingers to a wrist tight

Dig the nails deep into your palm and leave the marks

See the blood and still feel numb

While your hands shiver and body too

Oh dear! It's all the darkness of anxiety

Don't feel alone... I know the pain... So do many.

GOD'S PLA'

I loved him with all my heart and soul. So did he. We were the power couple, a sight to behold, walking hand in hand, our love untold. We lifted each other from the depths of despair, embracing the darkness and filling it with care, and looked after one another every minute. The beautiful thing happened behind the backs of our parents, who are two best friends.

How wonderful the feeling was when my father out of thin air asked me if I wanted to marry the man of my life. I jumped and screamed with happiness inside and showed no emotion. But answered, "As you wish." My father smiled and caressed my cheeks, and left the room.

But one day: "Not going to happen." my father signed with sadness and buried his face into his arms.

My stomach felt heavy, and my heart raced like a car in Formula 1. "What happened?" asked my mother. "The marriage of these two is not happening". "Because?" I jumped out of curiosity, fear, sadness or what-so-ever emotion that I doubt of.

"The horoscopes, the compatibility between you two are worse, and it's not happening." He finished and walked away.

"We have been together for the past many years and never felt a lack of compatibility." I wanted to say it out loud to my father, But no words escaped my lips, swallowed by the weight of the situation's eclipse.

Who knows if god planned to separate us in a bigger way when we were planning to convince our parents?

He left me by becoming a soulless body. He left me by becoming ashes and bones. He left me, the love of my life, the man of my dreams.

Though people say may he rest in peace, while I still suffer in silence and I wither, a little death within, as I mourn the loss of my forever love. It was like a nightmare when he bidded me a sweet goodbye and returned back into ashes. Little do I know how horrible this hurts.

WHEN THE...

When the seesaw stood still but the swings were dancing up and down.

When the slides were freezing cold.

When the sand turned snow.

When the cold breeze made our skin cold instead we were becoming hot; When his lips touched mine.

When the gift he said shall be given whenever we had a big fight.

When he shared the warmth of love through his lips.

When the place where I was upset became our meeting spot.

When we exchange each other's love for the first time and for an infinite time.

When you push a huge diamond ring.

When I cried out with happiness for the first time.

When we got tied together forever in the presence of the same seesaws, swings and slides.

When we took our kids and binded those memories.

When I sit in my 70s all alone, remember your broken promises of together forever.

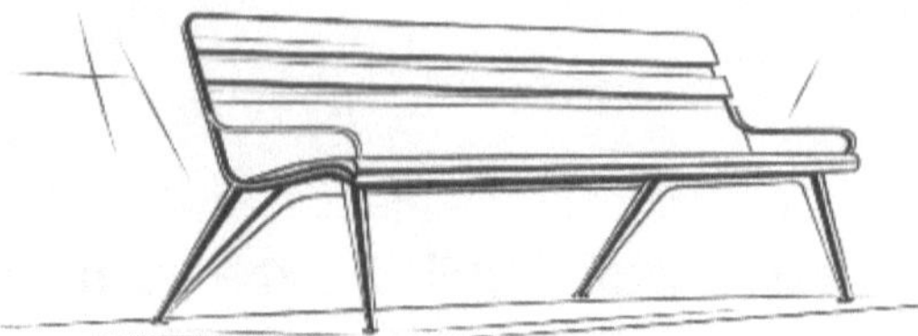

SWEET YOU!

The sweet smell of jasmine reminds me of the fragrance of your sweat.

The cold breeze reminds me of your soft touch.

The twinkling stars remind me of the shine in your eyes.

I can see everything around you except next to me.

Yes, my dear love! You are everywhere but way… far away.

RUN FOR THE RAINBOW

It was raining heavy

Yet the sun is peeking from the end...

The rays are hitting the clouds and making it into the tinted cheeks of the clouds...

Suddenly her legs stopped running in the corridors of her house as her eyes met the beautiful big rainbow…

She jumped in happiness. Leaving, all the pain of her tiny feet's restless run gone in thin air... She thought her search had come to an end...

Little does she know what the coming clouds are hiding for her… It's been 20

years... Still, the feet never stopped running while it was raining and sunning...

Still, she never stopped searching for the lime of the rainbows..... Leaving the tears back on her head...

She still smiles and jumps like a little girl..... Time has changed her a lot.But still, she kept her inner child alive.

RETURNED

We returned all the gifts we ever gave to each other.

We returned all the love we ever felt for each other.

We dumped off all the memories with each other.

But dear, you forgot to return back my heart that left a hole inside, that couldn't be filled.

SOMETIMES!

Sometimes it hurts more than before when you were actually suffering

Sometimes you get little heartaches which shovel a deep hole into your soul

Sometimes you miss to breath as it feels like you are in outer space

Sometimes it feels so heavy that rather than keeping it out, it puts you down.

PHOENIX

Little do I know that all the happy memories become nightmares....

Little do I know that my smile dies one day and becomes ashes....

Little do I know that one fine day I become a phoenix rising from my own ashes...

METAPHOR TO MY HEART

Tell me a metaphor for your heart right now, they say...

Just how the thunder hit the sky..... Bright and broken

Just how the dried earth looks.... Cracked and lifeless.

Just how you feel some nights.... Teary and crumbled!

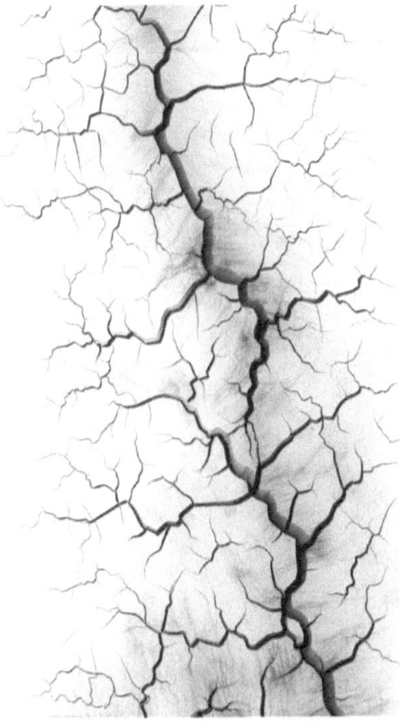

DEAR BLOOMER

To,

The storm inside the beds of a weeping flower which shows itself as a beauty to the world.

How is the weather inside you?

Have you ever asked yourself this question..... Maybe prioritising the weather of someone became more important to you that you let yourself drown and soak in the downpour of these heavy clouds. That you went unnoticed and now it's too late....

Never is late to get back on your feet and start building a boat and raft over to the

other end of the world where the shining sun peaks slow and calm like in a spring. Where the trees dance and sing for the wind. Where all the flowers bloom just for you.... You can still do it.

From,

A late bloomer.

PASSED

Trying to laugh a little bit and live my life a little bit. Ignoring the shit which bothers and accepting the past has passed.

Learning to seek help a little bit. Bounding to not go back to the people who left. Remembering the past has passed.

Jumping for self love and happiness. Being a little lazy is not my issue. Agreeing with the downfalls as miracles. And saying the past has passed.

It was these dark clouds which covered my mind

It was these dark clouds which made me nothing but numb

It was these dark clouds which made my vision blurred from the truth… and..

It was the heavy wind made them rain the pain and grief of restless thoughts

It was this downpour which cleansed her in and out

And finally it was the shine from the sun beneath which showed her path to her destiny.

INK OF SELF LOVE

It's all imprinted slow and deep,

like the foot in the sand set to sail,

In the ocean of salt it was just a speckle

The past all winded up and now begins

In the garden of self, roots intertwined,

Petals of self, unveiling day and day,

Nectar of flower, feels like yours

A story of self-love unfolds each.

The scars changes as the ink on the skin,

Embracing the evidence, where blooming begins,

Hard when pinning and alluring when done,

Oh, they'll be the story to tell to one.

A love so tender, past leaves no trace.

Soft as the first light, in your own embrace,

Beneath moonlight whispers, a love tale to unveil,

Is it the honey or the nectar of self?

Validation needs no more, in a world so loud,

the silence within, that can crown oneself.

Rise like the sun, from valleys below,

In the label of self-love, grow from rot.

In the pages of self, a poem like milk,

Lines of your love, in every heartbeat.

My ink whispers, a mirror to the soul,

In the language of self-love, find yourself whole.

UNVEILED

She was stabbed, more than she remembers

she was blamed, more than she knows,

she was played, more than she figured

she was cussed, more than she digested.

Was it a wake up call, when the life slipped

from the edge of the sleep-death,

it could be a life-call, where she realised

she breaths for herself.

Could it more accurate, the tip of her heels nails the
bygone,

when the paint on her nails tells the colour of their
vitals

the pawns of the chess hangs over her ears

and she is visible from the throne she laid her eyes
on.

Will she be the king or be the player

or make them sway under her layer

Not the god how needs to be the maker

but just her who makes it greater.

A BIG FLAG

It is the flag that coloured from blood

Makes all of them stop and stare.

I guess she is blind of colours or love

Can it define the way he loves?

Seeing her cuddle the bruises with smile

Look at her, look at her! Says the word to other

The heart on her sleeves covers everything

Where all he gets is the pecks and sex.

Was it the sun or was it the rain where all she knows
is to suffer in pain.

This time the hand and next goes the leash

When does he know that it's all insane?

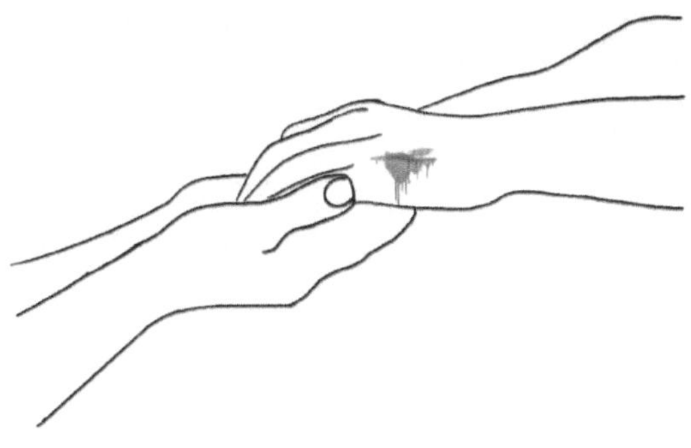

THE AISLE OF SOCIETY

Let not the pressure drown the inner voice,

the clock will tick, the seasons will pass,

a roller coaster of emotions plays around,

But let not the pressure dip you into the wrong one.

You crave for the better love, care and more

where all they see is scripted by tradition, veiled in societal light.

You walk on eggshells, even to pass through the way

where they want you to walk down the aisle.

Pressure mounts with every passing day,

To embark on a journey, the martial way.

You who know that it not yet the flight

all you seek is not to get it in vain.

WILT TO BLOOM

if you're wilting doesn't mean the end

It just means you have thousands of seedlings to make many bloom.

ECHOES OF LONGING

Did my care for you resonate enough?

Did my love for you radiate its warmth?

Have you ever yearned for a sorry or a hug,

To know you're still my dearest sister, my anchor snug?

Will the chance ever dawn to revive our bond,

To caress your delicate palms and peck on your cheeks respond?

A glimpse of you, a word or two to exchange,

The sweet slaps on my back, a connection to rearrange.

Why must the clock's ticking cease just for you?

Endless questions and cuddles are overdue.

Yet, one passionate wish echoes through the sky,

Return home, linger forever, my dear sister.

– Sami ♥

Follow me on Instagram: whisperingsoul2023

Get in touch: mahithaattili@gmail.com

www.ingramcontent.com/pod-product-compliance
Lightning Source LLC
Chambersburg PA
CBHW031329130726
47988CB00007B/3052